MW01143067

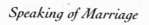

Speaking of Marriage

SPEAKING OF MARRIAGE

Edited by

CATHERINE GLASS

TEN SPEED PRESS
Berkeley, California

1☯
Ten Speed Press
P.O. Box 7123
Berkeley, California 94707

First printing, 1992

Copyright permissions can be found beginning on page 98.

Library of Congress Cataloging-in-Publication Data

Glass, Catherine.
    Speaking of marriage / [compiled by] Catherine Glass.
      p.   cm.
    ISBN 0-89815-433-2 :
    1. Marriage — Quotations, maxims, etc.   I. Title.
PN6084.M3G57   1992
392'.5 — dc20   91-4792
                                                          CIP

Printed in the United States of America

1   2   3   4   5   —   95   94   93   92

*To all those couples
courageously exploring the
country of marriage*

INTRODUCTION

In 1987, friends asked me to read quotations about marriage at their wedding. This was not the first marriage for either party, and naturally they expected something hopeful and profound as well as witty. I was happy to oblige and consulted the usual books of quotations, but to my dismay I found the sections on marriage filled with bitter and acerbic remarks by ancient and disillusioned writers.

Daunted but still game, I began to delve into my own library, fishing for quotations in books where I thought they might be lurking. This was a little like casting for the wily trout, but I managed to hook some good quotes and I read them with the bridegroom's best man to a crowd at the wedding. I was pleasantly surprised to find the reaction so positive, from the groom's twenty-year-old daughters to the bride's seventy-year-old parents. There were even requests for copies, and I found myself jotting down names and addresses over champagne and wedding cake.

In the ensuing years, I took note when a good marriage quotation surfaced. I had already noticed the curious fact that a state vital to the human condition was largely described by its detractors, so I began to celebrate when I found commentary that was genuinely helpful or even inspiring. Eventually, I saw my collection of quotations as a book, one with a realistic but positive point of view, one which described not only the pains of marriage and its comedy, but also its romance and joy.

I thank my friends and family for their support, particularly Julia Bergren, Jana McNulty, Pammette Riley, Charlie Sax, and Patrick Van Veen.

—CATHERINE GLASS

CONTENTS

ix

GREAT EXPECTATIONS

ome live with me, and be my love,

And we will some new pleasures prove

Of golden sands, and crystal brooks,

With silken lines, and silver hooks.

— JOHN DONNE

Marriage has many pains,

but celibacy has no pleasures.

—DR. SAMUEL JOHNSON

Hell! I'll never find another girl like this one. She's got everything I've ever looked for in a woman. She's beautiful, in bed and out. She's adventurous, brave, resourceful. She's exciting, always. She seems to love me. She'd let me go on with my life. She's a lone girl, not cluttered up with friends, relations, belongings. Above all, she needs me. It'll be someone for me to look after. I'm fed up with all these untidy, casual affairs that leave me with a bad conscience. I wouldn't mind having children. I've got no social background into which she would or wouldn't fit. We're two of a pair, really. Why not make it for always?

— JAMES BOND

*T*he men that women marry,
And why they marry them, will always be
A marvel and mystery to the world.

— HENRY WADSWORTH
LONGFELLOW

For two personalities to meet is like mixing two chemical substances. If there is any combination at all, both are transformed.

— CARL JUNG

When alkalis and acids meet, they grab each other, modify each other, and form a whole new substance. . . . In the same way, deep friendships develop between people who are opposites; opposite personalities are the best basis for a close union.

— JOHANN WOLFGANG
VON GOETHE

*O*ne old farmer giving me advice about choosing a wife once said, "Have a bloody good look at the mother first, lad," and I'm sure he had a point. But if I may throw in my own little word of counsel, it would be to have a passing glance at how she acts toward her father.

— JAMES HERRIOT

When the horoscopes of both partners show a harmonious constellation of the sun and the moon, their life together will be long and happy. The conjunction of a masculine moon with a feminine sun is very good for marriage.

— PTOLEMY

God is the great matchmaker.

—JEWISH PROVERB

Yes, I've given a lot of thought to marriage — that's why I'm single.

—PETER DE VRIES

It doesn't matter whether you decide to marry or stay single: either way you'll be sorry.

—SOCRATES

Marry and grow tame.

—SPANISH PROVERB

Marry and you may be sorry.
Don't, and you will be.

—CZECH PROVERB

*It is to be noticed that those
who have loved once or twice already
are so much the better educated.*

— ROBERT LOUIS STEVENSON

Lord, if we were all to marry our first loves what a plague of ill-assorted marriages there would be!

— GEORGETTE HEYER

I am not in favor of long engagements. They give people the opportunity of finding out each other's characters before marriage, which I think is never advisable.

— OSCAR WILDE

No one is perfect, and surely it is wiser to discover the imperfections before wedlock.

— E. M. FORSTER

Persons planning to embark on marriage should take a long trip together. The traumas of travel will tell them all they need to know about each other.

— RICHARD CAMAS

Marry in haste and be sorry at leisure.

—IRISH PROVERB

Hasty marriage seldom proveth well.

—WILLIAM SHAKESPEARE

In marriage do thou be wise: prefer the person before money, virtue before beauty, the mind before the body; then thou hast a wife, a friend, a companion, a second self.

—WILLIAM PENN

If you are considering marriage,
ask yourself one question:
will I still enjoy talking with her
when I'm old?

—FRIEDRICH NIETZSCHE

With thee conversing I forget all time,
All seasons and their change, all please alike.

—EVE, TO ADAM

*The Conversation of a Courtship is
more pleasing than ordinary Discourse.*

—SIR RICHARD STEELE

She is always married too soon
who gets a bad husband,
and she is never married too late
who gets a good one.

— DANIEL DEFOE

Now I want to be with my best friend,
and my best friend's my wife.
Who could ask for anything more?

— JOHN LENNON

Keep thy eyes wide open before marriage
and half-shut afterwards.

— BENJAMIN FRANKLIN

People who marry on sight are blind.

— GREEK PROVERB

If you want a good marriage,
marry your equal.

— OVID

*U*nequal matches are unlucky.

— RUSSIAN PROVERB

If she looked further than the wedding,
it was to see marriage as the beginning
of an individual existence; the skirmish
where one gained one's spurs,
from which one set out on the true
quests of life.

— EVELYN WAUGH

How delightful is your love, my sister, my
      bride!
   How much more pleasing is your love than
      wine,
   and the fragrance of your perfume than any
      spice!
Your lips drop sweetness as the honeycomb, my
      bride;
   milk and honey are under your tongue.
   The fragrance of your garments is like that of
      Lebanon.
You are a garden locked up, my sister, my
      bride;
   you are a spring enclosed, a sealed fountain.

        — SONG OF SOLOMON,
          4:10, 11 (NIV)

We longed to have no secrets from each other. We yearned for the courage to surrender ourselves. . . . You cannot imagine how much we hoped in the beginning.

— LIV ULLMANN

My simple opinion is that being in love is one thing, but marriage is not something to rush into. Marry only after you have reached a good understanding: then you will have a happy marriage. That is something that will benefit everyone, for happiness in the home and family leads ultimately to greater peace and happiness in the world.

—THE DALAI LAMA

How it starts is how it finishes.

—ENGLISH PROVERB

*I*n a Persian house, there is a wedding mirror, the breadth of two heads, framed in wrought silver. This is so because in Persian tradition it is the *union* of male and female which constitutes a human being. When the new husband and wife gaze into the mirror, they see in its oval not two human beings, but one.

— TERENCE O'DONNELL

What a Lover sees in the Beloved
is the projected shadow of his own
potential beauty in the eyes of God.

— COVENTRY PATMORE

. . . whither thou goest, I will go;
and where thou lodgest, I will lodge;
thy people shall be my people,
and thy God my God;
where thou diest, will I die,
and there will I be buried;
the Lord do so to me,
and more also, if aught but death
part thee and me.

      —THE BOOK OF RUTH 1:16–17

To have and to hold from this day forward,

for better for worse, for richer for poorer, in

sickness and in health, to love and to cherish,

till death us do part.

—BOOK OF COMMON PRAYER

That love is all there is
Is all we know of love.

— EMILY DICKINSON

Do anything rather than marry
without affection.

— JANE AUSTEN

COMEDY OF ERRORS

The antidote to love is marriage.

— CARADOS

Marriage from Love, like vinegar from wine —
A sad, sour, sober beverage — by Time
Is sharpened from its high celestial flavor
Down to a very homely household savor.

— LORD BYRON

Wives so often have excellent reasons for shooting
their husbands that one tends to suspect them
automatically.

— AGATHA CHRISTIE

The problem with marriage is that it ends every night after making love, and it must be rebuilt every morning before breakfast.

— GABRIEL GARCÍA MÁRQUEZ

. . . every love relationship is based on unwritten
conventions rashly agreed upon by the lovers during
the first weeks of their love. On the one hand,
they are living a sort of
dream; on the other, without realizing it, they are
drawing up the fine print of their contracts like the
most hard-nosed lawyers. O lovers! Be wary during
those perilous first days! If you serve the other party
breakfast in bed, you will be obliged to continue
same in perpetuity or face charges of
animosity and treason!

— MILAN KUNDERA

*Marriage indeed may qualify the fury
of his passion, but it very rarely mends
a man's manners.*

— WILLIAM CONGREVE

*It destroys one's nerves to be amiable
every day to the same human being.*

— BENJAMIN DISRAELI

*It is said that in marriage, the man and
woman give each other "his or her nethermost
beast" to hold. Each holds the leash for the
"nethermost beast" of the other.*

— ROBERT BLY

The country of marriage

has one peculiar characteristic —

strangers want to inhabit it

and its inhabitants want to flee.

— MICHEL MONTAIGNE

This incessant love, this unceasing spring. How boring! How tedious! Oh, for a tiny cloud, a little quarrel, a dilemma. I even considered taking a lover, just to cause some trouble!

—GEORGES FEYDEAU

arriage is one long conversation,
chequered by
disputes.

— ROBERT LOUIS STEVENSON

You can bear your own faults,
and why not a fault in your wife?

— BENJAMIN FRANKLIN

The rocks in his head fit the holes in hers.

—GORE VIDAL

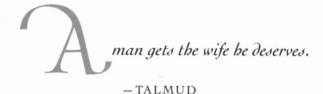

A *man gets the wife he deserves.*

—TALMUD

arrying a man is like buying something you've been admiring for a long time in a shop window. You may love it when you get it home, but it doesn't always go with everything else in the house.

— JEAN KERR

I tended to place my wife underneath a pedestal.

— WOODY ALLEN

Wives believe they've done everything when they love us: they love us and love us and are so incessantly obliging that one night we find to our surprise we are stuffed with love and all the happiness we hoped for has vanished.

— PIERRE AUGUSTIN
BEAUMARCHAIS

To have a discussion cooly waived when
you feel that justice is all on your own side
is even more exasperating in marriage than
in philosophy.

— GEORGE ELIOT

. . . I do think it surprising that any union should
survive the irritation of two separate personalities
impinging upon one another. One or the other is
usually top dog, and that must always be hard for
the underdog to accept.

— VITA SACKVILLE-WEST

When Hearts deserving Happiness would unite their fortunes, Virtue would crown them with an unfading garland of modest, hurtless flowers; but ill-judging Passion will force the gaudier Rose into the wreath, whose thorn offends them, when its leaves are dropt!

— RICHARD BRINSLEY SHERIDAN

. . . it's sometimes essential
for a husband and a wife to quarrel;
they get to know each other better.

—JOHANN WOLFGANG
VON GOETHE

I advise every husband:
answer your wife,
make her answer you.

—ISAK DINESEN

Husbands and wives generally understand
when opposition will be vain.

— JANE AUSTEN

Marriage might be called the capacity to finish
one another's sentences. I suspect it succeeds to
the degree that this capacity fails.

— AMANDA CROSS

*Silence
can be golden.*

—ANONYMOUS

A husband and wife should
avoid quarrels every-
where, but especially in bed.

— PLUTARCH

Those people who think good sex is more important to a marriage than good manners will find they are wrong. It is an irony, appreciated only by the French, that good manners are the basis of very good sex. In bed, the two most erotic words in any language are *thank you* and *please*.

— HUBERT DOWNS

Every experience is of value, and whatever one may say against marriage, it is certainly an experience.

— OSCAR WILDE

However perfect the honeymoon, the time will come, however brief it is, when you will wish she would fall downstairs and break a leg. That goes for her too. But the mood will pass, if you give it time.

— RAYMOND CHANDLER

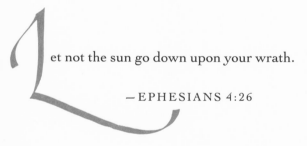

et not the sun go down upon your wrath.

— EPHESIANS 4:26

*E*nglish people of good position consider that

the basis of all marital unions or disunions is

the maxim: No scenes.

— FORD MADOX FORD

*he great secret of the successful marriage*

is to treat all disasters as incidents and

none of the incidents as disasters.

— HAROLD NICOLSON

Estimate her by the qualities she has, and not by the qualities she may not have. This is marriage.

—CHARLES DICKENS

. . . Alfred and I are happy, as happy as can be. We are in love, we are intellectually and physically suited in every possible way, we rejoice in each other's company, we have no money troubles and three delightful children. And yet, when I consider my life day by day, hour by hour, it seems to be composed of a series of pinpricks. . . . the endless drudgery of housekeeping, the nerve-racking noise and boring repetitive conversation of small children (boring in the sense that it bores into one's very brain), their absolute incapacity to amuse themselves, their sudden and terrifying illnesses, Alfred's not infrequent bouts of moodiness, his invariable complaints at meals about the pudding, the way he will always use my toothpaste and will squeeze the tube in the middle. These are the components of marriage, the wholemeal bread of life, rough, ordinary, but sustaining . . .

— NANCY MITFORD

The best marriages, like the best lives, were both happy and unhappy. There was even a kind of necessary tension, a certain tautness between the partners that gave the marriage strength, like the tautness of a full sail.

—ANNE MORROW LINDBERGH

Marriage can survive even the decline of physical passion if interests that are far more valuable take its place.

—HONORÉ DE BALZAC

Lord Illingworth: The Book of Life begins with a man
and a woman in a garden.

Mrs. Allonby: It ends with Revelations.

— OSCAR WILDE

One can't explain one's marriage.

— HENRY JAMES

Paradise Regained

When a man loves a woman

and that woman loves him,

the angels leave heaven and

come to their house and sing.

—BRAHMA

Marriage is like a garden.

It takes time.

— CARADOS

He was my husband. He was my lover.
He was my friend. He was my partner.
And he was an old soldier who
fought with me.

— YOKO ONO

No man knows what the wife
of his bosom is until he has gone with her through
the fiery trials of this world.

— WASHINGTON IRVING

There is nothing so fine as two people of one heart and mind keeping house together. They are the envy of their enemies and the delight of their friends.

— HOMER

The foundation of the family is the relationship between husband and wife. The tie that holds the family together lies in the loyalty and perseverance of the wife.

—I CHING

*Just as a cable is strengthened when inter-
twined, marriage is strengthened by the
goodwill contributed by each partner.*

— PLUTARCH

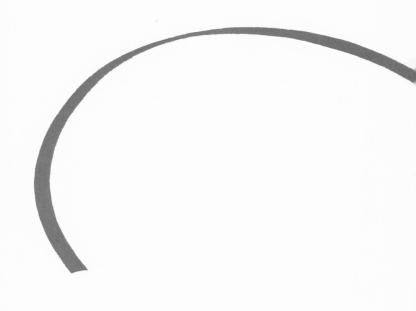

The value of marriage is not that adults produce children but that children produce adults.

— PETER DE VRIES

Like most human activities, love and marriage have little meaning without some sense of responsibility. It is the shared responsibility of working together as partners and in many cases bringing up children that creates a deeper joy. Relationships based on mutual understanding and respect, including compassion and kindness, become firmer, no matter how much time passes.

— THE DALAI LAMA

Marriage is a continuous process
and not a static condition. It is a plant
and not a piece of furniture.

— HAROLD NICOLSON

There is nothing more lovely in life than the union of two people whose love for one another has grown through the years from the small acorn of passion into a great rooted tree. Surviving all vicissitudes, and rich with its manifold branches, every leaf holding its own significance.

—VITA SACKVILLE-WEST

H ere I am, and here she is, and here we are. Now when I have to make a sacrifice, I'm not sacrificing to her, I'm sacrificing to the relationship.

— JOSEPH CAMPBELL

*G*ive your hearts, but not into each
    other's keeping.
For only the hand of Life can contain
    your hearts.
And stand together yet not too near
    together:
For the pillars of the temple stand apart,
And the oak tree and the cypress grow
    not in each other's shadow.

— KAHLIL GIBRAN

The Puritans called marriage "the little church within the Church." In marriage, every day you love, and every day you forgive. It is an ongoing sacrament — love and forgiveness.

— BILL MOYERS

Pay attention to the small child holding
     on to your hand,
And let your wife delight your heart.
For this is part of the destiny of man.

— SIDURI

*S*he felt that those enchantments which instinct had taught her to use would now make her appear ridiculous in the eyes of her husband, to whom from the very first moment she had surrendered herself with her whole soul, leaving not a single corner hidden from him. She felt that she was bound to her husband not by those poetic sentiments which had attracted him to her, but by something else, indefinite but indissoluble, which bound her own soul to her body.

— LEO TOLSTOY

It is easy to love when we feel that we are worthy of love, impossible otherwise.

— COVENTRY PATMORE

If thou lovest thyself, thou lovest thy wife.

— GEOFFREY CHAUCER

All loves lead to the final love, to the final stripping away of the unreal selves, to the true meeting. . . . It was such a miracle that it hardly mattered whether it was in first or second marriage, whether in youth or middle age. Whenever it happened, it was the true meeting, the true marriage.

— ANNE MORROW LINDBERGH

*V*oltaire

thought marriage was

the only adventure open to cowards.

But Voltaire never married,

or he would have known that marriage

requires a great deal of courage.

—HUBERT DOWNS

*When a man is intimate with his wife, the
longing of the eternal hills wafts about them.*

— MARTIN BUBER

*The uguisu on the flowering plum,
The stag beneath the autumn maple,
You and me together in bed,
Happy as two fish in water.*

— ANONYMOUS, JAPANESE

N.B. In Japanese, uguisu means bush warbler or nightingale.

I look at my husband's beloved body and I am very aware of the mystery of the Word made flesh, his flesh, the flesh of all of us, made potential.

— MADELEINE L'ENGLE

Let me not to the marriage of true minds
Admit impediments.

—WILLIAM SHAKESPEARE

. . . *to make One,* there must be Two . . .

— W. H. AUDEN

With my body I worship thee.

— MEDIEVAL MARRIAGE VOW

Wife, let us keep the tender names
    we first exchanged in our wedding bed;
And never let the days make us old.
    I'll be forever young for you,
    you, forever young for me.
When I'm as old as Nestor
    and you're older than the Delphic Sibyl,
Only the richness of the years will matter,
    not their number.

      —DECIMUS MAGNUS
      AUSONIUS

*I have never known what it was
to separate esteem from love.*

— JANE AUSTEN

Marriage, which has been the bourne of so many narratives, is still a great beginning, as it was to Adam and Eve, who kept their honeymoon in Eden, but had their first little one among the thorns and thistles of the wilderness. It is still the beginning of the home epic — the gradual conquest or irremediable loss of that complete union which makes the advancing years a climax, and age the harvest of sweet memories in common.

— GEORGE ELIOT

Love seems the swiftest, but it is the slowest of all growths. No man or woman really knows what perfect love is until they have been married a quarter of a century.

— MARK TWAIN

A happy marriage is a long conversation which always seems too short.

— ANDRÉ MAUROIS

But when two people are at one
    in their inmost hearts,
They shatter even the strength of iron
    or bronze.
And when two people understand each other
    in their inmost hearts,
Their words are sweet and strong,
    like the fragrance of orchids.

—I CHING

94

How but in custom and in ceremony
Are innocence and beauty born?

— WILLIAM BUTLER YEATS

No married couple can calculate the debt they
owe each other. It is an infinite sum and can
only be paid in eternity.

— JOHANN WOLFGANG
VON GOETHE

*Love shelters all things, trusts all things,
hopes all things, endures all things.*

—I CORINTHIANS 13:7

The deed of love is stronger than words.

— PEARL BAILEY

Love is often a fruit of marriage.

— JEAN-BAPTISTE MOLIÈRE

The painting featured throughout this book is *Flowers in a Silver Vase*, by Willem van Aelst, 1663. It is reproduced with permission of the Fine Arts Museums of San Francisco, Gift of Dr. and Mrs. Hermann Schuelein, 51.21.

INDEX OF FIRST LINES

Wilhelm and rendered into English by Cary F. Baynes. Bollingen Series XIX. Copyright © 1950, 1967 by Bollingen Foundation. Published by Princeton University Press, Princeton, N.J.

Come live with me,   [2]
From "The Bait" by John Donne, circa 1600.

Do anything rather than marry   [31]
From *Pride and Prejudice* by Jane Austen, 1813.

English people of good position   [56]
From *No More Parades* by Ford Madox Ford. Copyright © 1925 by Ford Madox Ford. Copyright © 1950 by Alfred A. Knopf, Inc. Reprinted by permission of Janice Biala, New York, and by permission of Alfred A. Knopf, Inc., New York.

Estimate her by the qualities she has,   [58]
From *David Copperfield* by Charles Dickens, 1849–50.

Every experience is of value,   [54]
From *The Portrait of Dorian Gray* by Oscar Wilde, 1890.

. . . every love relationship is based   [37]
From *The Book of Laughter and Forgetting* by Milan Kundera. Copyright © 1980 by Milan Kundera. Translated by Michael Heim. Reprinted by permission of Alfred A. Knopf, Inc., New York, and by Editions Gallimard, Paris.

For two personalities to meet   [6]
From *Psychological Reflections* by C. G. Jung. A New Anthology of

His Writings, edited by Jolande Jacobi and R. F. C. Hull.
Copyright © 1970 by the Bollingen Foundation. Bollingen Series
XXXI. Published by Princeton University Press.

Give your hearts, but not   [77]

From *The Prophet* by Kahlil Gibran. Copyright © 1923 by Kahlil
Gibran and renewed 1951 by Administrators C.T.A. of Kahlil
Gibran Estate and Mary G. Gibran. Reprinted by permission of
Alfred A. Knopf, Inc., New York.

God is the great matchmaker.   [9]

Jewish proverb.

Hasty marriage seldom proveth well.   [15]

From *Henry VI, Part III*, by William Shakespeare, 1590–92.

He was my husband. He was my lover.   [68]

From *Imagine John Lennon*, written and edited by Andrew Solt and
Sam Egan. Copyright © 1988 by Warner Bros., Inc., Yoko Ono,
and Sarah Lazin Book. Reprinted by permission of Macmillan
Publishing Company, New York.

Hell! I'll never find another girl   [4]

From *On Her Majesty's Secret Service* by Ian Fleming. Reprinted by
permission of © Gildrose Publications Ltd. 1963 and by permission
of Penguin USA, New American Library Signet edition, © 1963.

Here I am, and here she is,   [76]

From *The Power of Myth* by Joseph Campbell & Bill Moyers.
Copyright © 1988 by Apostrophe S Productions, Inc. and Bill
Moyers and Alfred Van der Marck Editions, Inc. for itself and the

estate of Joseph Campbell. Reprinted by permission of Doubleday, a division of Bantam Doubleday Dell Publishing Group, Inc., New York.

How but in custom and in ceremony   [95]

From "Prayer for My Daughter" in *Collected Poems of William Butler Yeats*. Copyright © 1924 by Macmillan Publishing Company, renewed 1952 by Bertha Georgie Yeats. Reprinted by permission of Macmillan Publishing Company, New York.

How delightful is your love,   [23]

From Song of Solomon 4:10, 11, circa 1000–600 B.C. Reprinted from the Holy Bible, New International Version. Copyright © 1973, 1978, 1984 International Bible Society. Reprinted by permission of Zondervan Bible House, all rights reserved, and by permission of Hodder & Stoughton Ltd., London.

How it starts is how it finishes.   [27]

English proverb.

However perfect the honeymoon,   [55]

From a letter from Raymond Chandler to Neil Morgan, November 18, 1955. Reprinted by permission of Neil Morgan, San Diego, CA.

Husbands and wives generally understand when   [50]

From *Persuasion* by Jane Austen, 1818.

I advise every husband: [49]

From *Daguerreotypes* by Isak Dinesen. Translated by P. M. Mitchell and W. D. Paden. Copyright © 1979 by the Rungstedlund

Foundation. Reprinted by permission of the University of Chicago Press, Chicago, IL.

I am not in favor of long engagements.   [13]
From *The Importance of Being Ernest* by Oscar Wilde, 1895.

. . . I do think it surprising that any union   [47]
From *No Signposts in the Sea* by Vita Sackville-West. Copyright © 1961 by Vita Sackville-West. Published by Michael Joseph, London, and by Doubleday. Reprinted by permission of Doubleday, a division of Bantam Doubleday Dell Publishing Group, Inc., New York and with the kind assistance of Virago Press, London.

I have never known what it was to separate   [90]
From *Sense and Sensibility* by Jane Austen, 1811.

I look at my husband's beloved body   [85]
From *Two-Part Invention: The Story of a Marriage* by Madeleine L'Engle. Copyright © 1988 by Crosswicks, Ltd. Reprinted by permission of Farrar, Straus & Giroux, Inc., and by permission of Lescher & Lescher, Ltd., New York.

I tended to place my wife underneath a pedestal.   [45]
Reprinted by permission of Woody Allen.

If she looked further than the wedding,   [22]
From *Brideshead Revisited: The Sacred and Profane Memories of Captain Charles Ryder* by Evelyn Waugh. Copyright © 1944, 1945 by Evelyn Waugh. Copyright © renewed 1972, 1973 by Mrs. Laura Waugh. Reprinted by permission of Little, Brown & Company, Boston, and by permission of Peters Fraser & Dunlop Group, Ltd., London.

If thou lovest thyself,   [81]
  From *The Canterbury Tales* by Geoffrey Chaucer, 1393–1400.

If you are considering marriage,   [17]
  From *Human, All Too Human* by Friedrich Nietzsche, 1878.
  Rendered into English by Catherine Glass © 1991.

If you want a good marriage,   [21]
  From *Heroides* by Ovid, written sometime after 43 B.C. and before
  8 A.D. Translated by Catherine Glass © 1991.

In a Persian house,   [28]
  Reprinted by permission of Terence O'Donnell. See also
  O'Donnell's *Garden of the Brave in War*, published by the University
  of Chicago.

In marriage do thou be wise: [16]
  From *Some Fruits of Solitude* by William Penn, 1693.

It destroys one's nerves to be amiable   [38]
  From *The Young Duke* by Benjamin Disraeli, 1831.

It doesn't matter whether you decide to marry   [11]
  From *The Lives and Opinions of Eminent Philosophers* by Diogenes
  Laertius (sometimes called Laertius Diogenes) circa 200–240 A.D.
  Translated by Catherine Glass © 1991.

It is easy to love when we feel that   [81]
  From *The Rod, the Root and the Flower* by Coventry Patmore, 1895.

Lord, if we were all to marry our first loves   [13]

From *A Civil Contract* by Georgette Heyer. Copyright © by
Georgette Heyer 1961. Copyright renewed by Richard George
Rougier 1989. Reprinted by permission of Heron Enterprises Ltd.
Mandarin Books (UK)/Harper Paperbacks (USA).

Love is often a fruit   [97]

From *Sganarelle* by Jean-Baptiste Molière, 1660.

Love seems the swiftest,   [92]

From *Mark Twain's Notebook*, edited and with comments by Albert
Bigelow Paine. Copyright © 1935 by The Mark Twain Company.
Reprinted by permission of HarperCollins Publishers, New York.

Love shelters all things, trusts all things   [96]

From 1 Corinthians 13:7, New Testament, circa 54 A.D. Translated
by Catherine Glass © 1991.

Marriage can survive even the decline of   [61]

From *The Memoirs of Two Young Wives* by Honoré de Balzac, 1830.
Translated by Catherine Glass © 1991.

Marriage from Love, like vinegar from wine —   [35]

From *Don Juan* by Lord Byron, 1819–22.

Marriage has many pains,   [3]

From *Rasselas, Prince of Abyssinia* by Dr. Samuel Johnson, 1759.

Marriage indeed may qualify the fury   [38]

From *Love for Love* by William Congreve, 1695.

Marrying a man is like buying something   [44]
> From *The Snake Has All the Lines* by Jean Kerr. Copyright © 1960 by
> Jean Kerr. Reprinted by permission of Doubleday, a division of
> Bantam Doubleday Dell Publishing Group, Inc., New York.

My simple opinion is that being in love   [25]
> The Dalai Lama in an essay sent to Catherine Glass, May 1991.
> Copyright © 1991, the Dalai Lama, Himachal Pradesh.

No man knows what the wife of his bosom is   [68]
> From *The Sketch Book (of Geoffrey Crayon, Gent)* by Washington
> Irving, 1819–20.

No married couple can calculate   [95]
> From *Elective Affinities* by Johann Wolfgang von Goethe, 1809.
> Rendered into English by Catherine Glass © 1991.

No one is perfect,   [13]
> From *A Room with a View* by E. M. Forster. Copyright © 1908 by
> E. M. Forster. Reprinted from a Vintage Books edition © 1986 by
> permission of Alfred A. Knopf, New York, and by permission of
> Hodder & Stoughton Publishers Ltd./New English Library, Ltd./
> Edward Arnold, London and Kent, England.

Now I want to be with my best friend,   [19]
> From *Imagine John Lennon*, written and edited by Andrew Solt and
> Sam Egan. Copyright © 1988 by Warner Bros. Inc., Yoko Ono, and
> Sarah Lazin Book. Reprinted by permission of Macmillan
> Publishing Company, New York.

Silence can be golden.   [51]
> Anonymous philosopher discussing marriage.

That love is all there is   [31]
> From Poem 1765 by Emily Dickinson in *The Complete Poems of Emily Dickinson*, edited by Thomas H. Johnson. Copyright © 1914, 1942 by Martha Dickinson Bianchi. Published by Little, Brown & Company, Boston.

The antidote to love   [34]
> From *The Dufek Intrusion* by Catherine Glass © 1991.

The best marriages, like the best lives,   [60]
> From *Dearly Beloved* by Anne Morrow Lindbergh. Copyright © 1962 by Anne Morrow Lindbergh and renewed 1990 by Anne M. Lindbergh. Reprinted by permission of Harcourt Brace Jovanovich, Inc., Orlando, FL.

The Book of Life begins   [63]
> From *A Woman of No Importance* by Oscar Wilde, 1893.

The Conversation of a Courtship   [18]
> From *The Englishman*, 9,57, by Sir Richard Steele, 1713.

The country of marriage   [40]
> From *Essays* by Michel Eyquem de Montaigne, 1580–95. Translated by Catherine Glass © 1991.

The deed of love   [97]

From "First and Last," June 19, 1989 *New Yorker* profile of Louis Belsen by Whitney Balliet. Pearl Bailey to Whitney Balliet. Copyright © 1989 by Whitney Balliet. Reprinted by permission of *The New Yorker*, New York.

The foundation of the family   [70]

From the *I Ching*, circa 1150 B.C. with commentaries by Confucius, circa 500 B.C., and by Wang Pi, circa 225 A.D. Translated by Richard Wilhelm and rendered into English by Cary F. Baynes. Bollingen Series XIX. Copyright © 1950, 1967 by Bollingen Foundation. Published by Princeton University Press, Princeton, N.J.

The great secret to the successful marriage   [57]

From a 1929 BBC program featuring Harold Nicolson and Vita Sackville-West. According to Nicolson's biographer, Mr. Nicolson actually said, "I think the secret of a successful marriage is the capacity to treat disasters as if they were incidents and not to magnify incidents into disasters," but oral tradition passed the quote to posterity as it appears in our text.

The men that women marry,   [5]

From "Michael Angelo" by Henry Wadsworth Longfellow, 1883.

The problem with marriage   [36]

From *Love in the Time of Cholera* by Gabriel García Márquez. Copyright © 1988 by Gabriel García Márquez. Translated by Edith Grossman. Reprinted by permission of Alfred A. Knopf, Inc., New York.

The Puritans called marriage   [78]

> From *The Power of Myth* by Joseph Campbell & Bill Moyers.
> Copyright © 1988 by Apostrophe S Productions, Inc. and Bill
> Moyers and Alfred Van der Marck Editions, Inc. for itself and the
> estate of Joseph Campbell. Reprinted by permission of Doubleday,
> a division of Bantam Doubleday Dell Publishing Group, Inc., New
> York.

The rocks in his head fit the holes in hers.   [43]

> Reprinted by permission of Gore Vidal.

The uguisu on the flowering plum,   [84]

> From an anonymous Japanese poem translated by Kenneth Rexroth
> in *One Hundred More Poems from the Japanese*. Copyright © 1976 by
> Kenneth Rexroth. Reprinted by permission of New Directions
> Publishing Corporation, New York.

The value of marriage is not that adults   [72]

> From *The Tunnel of Love* by Peter De Vries. Copyright © 1949 by
> Peter De Vries. Reprinted by permission of Little, Brown &
> Company, Boston.

There is nothing more lovely in life   [75]

> From *No Signposts in the Sea* by Vita Sackville-West. Copyright ©
> 1961 by Vita Sackville-West. Published by Michael Joseph,
> London, and by Doubleday. Reprinted by permission of Doubleday,
> a division of Bantam Doubleday Dell Publishing Group, Inc., New
> York, and with the kind assistance of Virago Press, London.

There is nothing so fine as two people of one heart   [69]

> From *The Odyssey* by Homer, circa 800 B.C. Translated by Catherine
> Glass © 1991.

New York, and by permission of George Weidenfeld & Nicolson Limited, London.

What a lover sees in the Beloved   [28]
From *The Rod, the Root and the Flower* by Coventry Patmore, 1895.

When a man is intimate with his wife,   [84]
From *I and Thou* by Martin Buber. Translated by Ronald Gregor Smith. Copyright © 1958 by Charles Scribner's Sons. Reprinted by permission of Charles Scribner's Sons, an imprint of Macmillan Publishing Company, New York, and by permission of T&T Clark Ltd., Publishers, Edinburgh.

When a man loves a woman   [66]
From sayings attributed to Brahma. Rendered into English by Catherine Glass © 1991.

When alkalis and acids meet,   [6]
From *Elective Affinities* by Johann Wolfgang von Goethe, 1809. Rendered into English by Catherine Glass © 1991.

When Hearts deserving Happiness   [48]
From *The Rivals* by Richard Brinsley Sheridan, 1777.

When the horoscopes of both partners   [8]
From *Opera Omnia V* by Ptolemy, circa 100–151 A.D. Translated by Catherine Glass © 1991.

. . . whither thou goest, I will go;   [29]
From Book of Ruth 1:16–17, circa 400 B.C. Holy Bible, King James Version, 1611.

Speaking of Marriage

DESIGNED BY NANCY AUSTIN.
COMPOSED BY WILSTED & TAYLOR, OAKLAND, CA,
IN LINOTYPE COCHIN WITH DISPLAY LETTERS
FROM "ARTHUR BAKER'S COPYBOOK OF RENAISSANCE
CALLIGRAPHY" BY DOVER PUBLICATIONS.
THE ETCHINGS ARE FROM VARIOUS RENAISSANCE
SOURCES. THE PAINTING IS "FLOWERS IN A SILVER
VASE" BY WILLEM VAN AELST, 1663.